IMMORTAL

WHISPERS

Spiritual Poetry

NINA KHAJURIA

JOYFUL LIFE MASTERY BOOKS

Copyright © 2022 by Nina Khajuria

ISBN: 978-1-990669-06-4

All rights reserved. No part of this publication may be reproduced, distributed, or transmitted in any form or by any means, including photocopying, recording, or other electronic or mechanical methods, without the prior written permission of Joyful Life Mastery, except by a reviewer, who may quote brief passages in a review.

I offer this book to Sri Sathya Sai Baba.
My source of inspiration, grace and compassion.
For the many Acharyas, Siddhas, and Saints to whom
I have had the privilege of spending valuable time
receiving their blessings, I offer my deepest respects.

Table of Contents

Immortal Sound 1

Walking Fool 3

Ahimsa 4

Birds In Motion 6

Beloved 10

Forgetting My Soul 12

Sunshine 13

Ocean Blue 15

Divine Teacher 17

Melody 20

Wayside Traveller	22
Awaken	23
Melody II	25
Hilltop	27
Hush, Ego Hush	29
Let Me Be	33
The Gatekeeper	37
Sai Darshan	40
Dive Deep	43
Arise	46
Thank you	49
About The Author	51
About The Book	53

Immortal Sound

You are silent deep down in my heart.

No, within every fibre in my body.

When in agony and misery,

you sing lullabies in my heart.

When I am happy,

you make me sing and dance.

In contemplation,

your effulgence

        unveils who I Am.

The Ancients called you OM.

The sound, Immortal.

Walking Fool

Fool, you are walking

Thoughts, your companion

    Stop

Watch the multicolored flowers

Yellow, red, crimson

Petals unfolding as the sun goes by

Learn their mysteries

Unity in diversity

Ahimsa

I believe in Ahimsa.

Yet I do not know what it is.

I hold bad thoughts.

I feel vengeance when I am hurt.

I listen to stories untrue that my Neighbor spreads.

I am jealous of another's success.

I revel in my opponent's failure.

Tirthankaras and Avatars announced,

time and time again,

these are Himsa.

Weak as I am,

I fall back into the dark pit.

Birds In Motion

I strolled along

the southern beach.

I saw a multitude of birds,

their colors, magnificent.

A bird chirped.

Friend, from where does thou hail? I asked.

A lonely bird replied,

it's sad, a tale.

I hail from the northern mountains,

where trees are tall and strong,

flowers red and yellow,

streams bouncing merrily along,

the mighty ocean holding forth.

Friend, the snow comes with time.

So, we fly south,

for food and shelter,

in groups large and small.

    Circling

    dancing

    chasing

Alas, a mountain fire

swallowed a few.

Dozens gasped for air,

and died in a crowded city,

engulfed in smoke and fog.

Weep not, dear friend.

Pray they are born again.

Humans mighty, fortune aplenty.

Make a healthy world!

For love and harmony,

for land, water, sky and mountains.

Rejoice in a new tomorrow.

Beloved

I know a thief is hiding my beloved,
thought the culprit.

Dancing, dazzling,
new and old stories,
some painful, some happy.
    clouding
        silence
            peace within

Covering this lover of mine.

Time is here and now.
                        Destroy its tentacles.

Merge with my lover,
the one and only one.

He and I are one and the same.

Forgetting My Soul

Friend, I bartered

a precious gem in the market place.

I exchanged the purity within.

Ego moved through family, friends,

All.

Desire, ambition reigned.

Forgetting my Soul,

my precious love.

He and I are one.

Sunshine

I walked up the peak of success.

A crown for a helmet, honor adorned.

I searched for peace and purity within.

Yet there was only emptiness,

darkness.

I cried in vain.

Sunshine

I heard a voice calm and sweet,

deep down in the valley,

where you left them.

Ocean Blue

Standing by the ocean calm and blue

Wandering secrets

beheld in its dark bosom

The mighty ocean roared, laughing

Water rose high,

Gentle waves cooling my weary feet

Friend shake your heart

Let the troubling thoughts rush out

Let the effulgent light shine within

I take all the waters into my bosom

Dark and clear, dancing in ecstasy

Wonder not the everchanging

Search for the ever existing

Divine Teacher

Tell me, friend.

Why do troubles unknown,

come like a sudden cloud

ready to burst?

Why do I kneel and pray?

I have no guilt.

I have nothing hidden.

I may have forgotten

words and deeds,

to remember my love.

Lord, why send your

Angel of Troubles?

I walked the path

of righteousness,

truth,

honesty.

The banner is mine.

I know your play

at the banks of the Jamuna.

Dancing, teasing.

My lord smiled.

Troubles came your way

From actions and reactions past.

I carried you through it

in my arms.

My arms above you,

my arms below you,

shielding every blow,

guiding every step.

Melody

The enemies within awaken.

A cloud of darkness spreads.

Consciousness and tranquility are

drowned in sorrow.

    Eyes blinded with weary tears,

    fear and doubt crawl in.

Emotions take wing, hither and thither.

　　　　　Days are spent

　　　searching for the light.

　　　The citadel of peace.

I heard a sound within my soul.

It was my lover, the flute player.

The melodies,

　　　　　　　deep

deep within my heart

Wayside Traveller

I am a wayside traveller.
I live here and there,
by brooks and streams.
I eat with the unchaste.

I laugh with the wicked.
I have many mothers.
I have many fathers.
I travelled the weary road many a time.
I am still a wayside traveller.

Awaken

I am awake from the slumber.

I reached the banks of Jordan,

or Ganges.

Whatever they may be called.

I search for the golden light.

I climb the pious mountain.

One the rishis and sages sanctified.

I greet yogis donning matted hair.

Beard to the floor,

as they sit in deep silence.

Awaiting the hour God awakens.

No.

No, the God you love,

is awake within.

Search no more.

Melody 11

In the dark days of my life,

I cried alone.

Fear and death,

my sole companions.

Abandoned by friends,

tranquility deserted.

Amidst it all,

I heard a flute within.

Playing a melody,

sweetly comforting.

My lover, is there,

in the depths of my heart.

Hilltop

My love told me to meet Him,

at the peak of the hill,

where the sun never sets.

And effulgence, tranquility,

eternity, truth, love,

will always be mine.

I started walking.

> Yet wayside, I was dazzled.

Richness and ambition beckoned to me.

Pleasure and gratification greeted me.

> Forgetting my lover on the hill top.

Hush, Ego, Hush

Hush, ego, hush.

Remember the days gone by.

Enshrouded hopes,

unknown, unfathomable darkness.

Fear everywhere.

The unfortunate ones.

Seek hither and thither,

knocking on different doors

some doomed,

some misleading.

Hush, ego, hush.

The time to smile is not afar.

The doors will open.

Search deep.

Open the doors.

And embrace the faith.

Frightened, anywhere, everywhere.

Not aware of when and where,

you lost your beloved soul.

Behind locked doors,

yearning, weeping.

Yes, the door opened.

The vision came.

The unfortunate ones seeking,

hither and thither,

knocking on different doors.

Some doomed, some misleading.

Hush ego, hush ego.

The time to smile is not afar.

The doors will open when they search

deep within their hearts.

Let Me Be

Spring sprang,

laughing in delight,

spreading flowers in multitude.

Perhaps offering obeisance

to mother earth.

Safeguarding the dark winter

in her mighty womb.

Perhaps offering salutations

to the sun.

Gentle rays,

awakening from the long slumber.

I bent down slowly to enjoy the beauty

of a blossoming flower.

She shifted slowly,

whispering gently.

Halt.

Touch me not, if you may.

The human touch is painful,

destroying identity and values.

They smother me a day.

Maybe pass me to another,

for services expecting or rendered.

They trade kith and foe

in the marketplace.

Muttering...

Profit is mine,

vengeance is my currency.

Halt friend, if you may.

Let me be another day,

saluting the great ones.

Let me whisper to the gentle breeze...

Love and peace to all mankind.

The Gatekeeper

The darkness enveloped me.

Rain slashed down pitilessly,

the angry sky streaming a terrifying light.

Thunder echoed,

shaking earth and heaven.

I covered my face and wept deeply.

No friends, no kith and no kin to comfort me.

Lo and behold, I heard a gentle knock

at the door of my heart.

Trembling, I said, who are you?

A soft voice murmured,

I am your gate keeper.

I am the guiding light within you,

guarding time immemorable.

I was your playmate in the garden of Babylon.
I was your protector in Nalanda.
I was your love in Vrindavan.

I shielded you from every blow from the wicked and immoral.
I heard you in your agony.

With every sob, I wiped your tears each and every time.
I am the guiding light,
bright within your heart.

💜

Sai Darshan

The Divine Supreme

came at different times,

into different religions

with a ray of sunshine,

a touch of knowledge.

To lead you and me

from the unreal to the real.

Alas, you and I,

still chant empty words

in their names.

                Awaken.

It is time

to follow the light,

to digest their words,

and reach the ultimate.

The infinite - the Knowledge

shining in your heart.

    Follow, follow the messages,

        the treasures they left.

    Awaken the knowledge within.

Dive Deep

Dive deep,

deep within.

Reach peace, divine.

Beauty is faith.

Faith is beauty.

Keep the guiding star in sight.

Forget not the precious gems,

determination,

    and persistence.

Dive deep, deep within you.

Wisdom shines the brightest within the depths of darkness.

Remember the divine with every step,

in every hour.

Walk with faith, your head held high.

Rise above doubts or discrimination, cast or creed.

Stop not by the wayside puddles to quench your thirst.

Reach the nectar deep within you.

    Dive deep,

    deep within.

Arise

Awaken, my friend.

The bright sun beckons.

Happiness and friendship are in the air.

    The lonely heart

    harbors Darkness.

    Let the light shine within.

Brush away

doubts and sadness.

Do not dwell on the sad past.

The future is bright.

Unlock happiness

deep within.

You alone hold the key.

Flood your heart.

Be bright and happy.

Hope and purity

shine within.

The world awaits

with open arms.

Arise. Smile.

Smile.

Come friend, let us walk.

Hand in hand, in the sun. ☼

With a smile on our lips.

And cheer in our hearts. 💗

Thank you

For their sense of duty, spirituality, and daily support, I wish to acknowledge...

My husband Ramesh and my daughters Priya and Kavita.

My beautiful granddaughter Janaki, who tries to change the world with her art and designs.

My beautiful granddaughter Sundari, whose love is always a fragrance.

Ken Davies, my son-in-law, a dedicated husband and father who is always ready to help me with everything computer-related.

Smt Lilavanti Khajuria, my mother-in-law, whose life-practice and deep faith in Jainism inspired me to study and research Jainism, and who is always in our hearts.

With affectionate recognition to Aneli Khajuria, my sister-in-law, who holds on to the family and faith with deep strength in the face of adversity, and is always an inspiration.

I would like to extend my special thanks to my daughter Priya Khajuria for her assistance in editing and publishing this book.

About The Author

Nina Khajuria is the author of *Human Values in Jainism* (2005, Paper Print Services, Mumbai, India).

She studied law in London, U.K. and at McGill University in Montreal, Canada. She taught law at Holborn College of Law in London, England and practiced law in the United Kingdom. In Vancouver, Canada, Nina worked at the Attorney General's office as a consultant and traveled across British Columbia as part of a team.

Nina stayed at the Sathya Sai Baba Ashram in India for 7 years and was a frequent visitor to the Divine Life Society in Uttar Pradesh. She has traveled to

Gangotri in the Himalayas and stayed at ashrams, participating and visiting monks in meditation.

On her return to Canada, Nina taught at Simon Fraser University for a short period and did social work as a Board member of the Heart and Stroke Foundation of British Columbia, and as the Vice Chair on the Race Relations Board in Vancouver.

Nina is now busy reading, researching and writing spiritual and related subjects. She enjoys traveling with her husband and family.

About The Book

All proceeds from sales of this book will be donated to *The Dream Project*.

The Dream Project is a collaboration between the Los Angeles County Department of Mental Health and the Jain Community, which was organized by Dr. Nitin Shah and facilitated by Dr. Kavita Khajuria.

It aims to provide assistance to the disadvantaged.

www.ingramcontent.com/pod-product-compliance
Lightning Source LLC
Chambersburg PA
CBHW071409070526
44578CB00002B/530